SEASONS FOR YOUR SOUL:

Poems with Purpose

SHEILA COX GAGEN

WestBow Press books may be ordered through booksellers or by contacting:

WestBow Press
A Division of Thomas Nelson & Zondervan
1663 Liberty Drive
Bloomington, IN 47403
www.westbowpress.com
844-714-3454

Because of the dynamic nature of the Internet, any web addresses or links contained in this book may have changed since publication and may no longer be valid. The views expressed in this work are solely those of the author and do not necessarily reflect the views of the publisher, and the publisher hereby disclaims any responsibility for them.

Any people depicted in stock imagery provided by Getty Images are models, and such images are being used for illustrative purposes only.
Certain stock imagery © Getty Images.

Scripture quotations taken from The Holy Bible, New International Version® NIV® Copyright © 1973 1978 1984 2011 by Biblica, Inc. TM. Used by permission. All rights reserved worldwide.

Scripture taken from the New King James Version® Copyright © 1982 by Thomas Nelson. Used by permission. All rights reserved.

Photo credits: Lisa Miller, Sarah Taylor, Elaine Potter, and Sheila Gagen.

ISBN: 978-1-6642-5450-3 (sc)
ISBN: 978-1-6642-5451-0 (e)

Library of Congress Control Number: 2022903617

Print information available on the last page.

WestBow Press rev. date: 2/22/2022

WESTBOW
PRESS®
A DIVISION OF THOMAS NELSON
& ZONDERVAN

In loving memory of

Mom and Dad

these poems came alive during your lifetime
and like your memory and love will live on
as you continue to Praise the Lord in heaven, forevermore.

SUMMER 1

"This is what the L<small>ORD</small> says:
'Stand at the crossroads and look;
ask for the ancient paths,
ask where the good way is, and walk in it,
and you will find rest for your souls.'"
Jeremiah 6:16 NIV

I will provide

Stay with Me,
I will provide,
I am every good and nourishing kind,
all that you dread
will be goodness instead
until there's no memory of what
it was you wished it would be...
Stay with Me,
I will provide,
nothing's allowed that lives outside,
Hope is fulfilled
where there's only My will.
Stay with Me,
I will provide,
all evil will have died
and you couldn't recall it even if you tried;
it's more than being satisfied,
it's how life was meant to be –
stay with Me.

SUMMER 2

*"Whoever believes in me,
as Scripture has said,
streams of living water will
flow from within him."*
John 7:38 NIV

There will be peace in Your presence
flowing pure with delight
filling us with your refreshing
as you carry our sorrows out of our sight.
We long to drink of Your living water,
freely it will never cease,
we who are errant sons and daughters
finally resting in Your peace.
There we will have no burdens,
You wash them away in Your gentle stream
our thirst will suddenly be no more
and our souls, sparkling clean.
Draw me closer
to hear the sound
of Your peaceful presence
streaming down
and know in my spirit that You are near
Jesus, shelter me,
with Your presence here.

SUMMER 3

There's a brave little flower
with scant water
on its own,
receiving less of love,
yet still it's shown
that even when thrown
upon a heap
has brought itself
to dig down deep
though early expectations
were low,
in the beginning,
it still managed to grow
and now discovered
by a discerning eye
gives its brave, beautiful essence
inspiring all
who would pass it by.

*"God did this so that men would seek him
and perhaps reach out for him and find him,
though he is not far from each one of us."*
Acts 17:27 NIV

SUMMER 4

"You make known to me the path of life:
You will fill me with joy in your presence,
with eternal pleasures at your right hand."
Psalm 16:11 NIV

I saw a glimmer
then a glimpse
of a shaft of sunshine
on the path it lit
and couldn't help but
follow through
to the place
it led me to,
and all the while
the feeling
clear,
I was at peace
and supposed
to be here,
free from strife
and free from fear,
I cross the bridge
down a peaceful path
in faith, disappear...

SUMMER 5

"Let the morning bring me word
of your unfailing love,
for I have put my trust in you.
Show me the way I should go,
for to you I lift up my soul."
Psalm 143:8 NIV

We see what man has made
but it's the sunrise
that takes our breath away;
we have our sons and daughters
but it's blue waters
that remain;
so where are we in all this frame?
That God is greater
and His Name
will last forever
He is the same;
thus we know that we are now,
but God forever,
will reign.

Morning glory
be to You
oh Maker of creation story
who,
brings boundless beauty in this way
awaken our appreciation
of the Lord of endless days.
Snow and sun
sing the Holy One,
to raise
our souls and minds to You,
if only for a day,
in the way,
of awe
that will be to You ablaze
forever in Heaven
with our eternal praise.

SUMMER 6

"Where morning dawns and evening fades
you call forth songs of joy."
Psalm 65:8 NIV

On Monday mornings we would rise,
To amber meadows, azure skies,
And hear the still, small voice inside
So silent is the dawn.

With work no farther than our door,
Asking little; receiving more.
Not knowing whether rich or poor-
Content with what we have.

We'd live God's time –By sun and moon
All else is later, now, or soon.
No ticking clocks say "nine" or "noon"-
No measurement of time.

By evening, filtered golden rays
Of sunlight slant through radiant haze
And house lights twinkle as twilight fades-
God grant us simpler times.

SUMMER 7

"And let the beauty of the Lord our God be upon us, And establish the work of our hands for us; Yes, establish the work of our hands."
Psalm 90:17 NKJV

Today I'm a butterfly
all sunshine and shade,
light as a cloud
floating where I may.
The field is my freedom,
my forage is play,
I dance on flowers' faces
as time has no say.
There exists only now,
I'll rise and I'll rest
with tranquilities wings
as one who is blessed...

the feathery weeds
are as silent chimes
playing with the wind,
sounding the times;
shall we not sit
in the Lord's repose
and give Him Glory
and compose
the songs of our heart
that please Him so much
when we are truly grateful
we know His loving touch

SUMMER 8

"Yet I am always with you;
you hold me by my right hand.
You guide me with your counsel,
and afterward you will take me into glory."
Psalm 73:23-24 NIV

those evenings,
after a long pleasant day,
when the sky turns blue
as the sun melts away
stillness descends
neither cold nor hot
just a feeling,
a measure,
of what it has brought
as though heaven were near
and I have been blessed
with a moment of waiting
in pure happiness

SUMMER 9

"Hope deferred makes the heart sick,
but a longing fulfilled is a tree of life."
Proverbs 13:12 NIV

What is that they say?
You can't see the forest
for the trees?
When those are gone,
what does it leave?
We're cutting down those
that only lie before us
until one day there will be
no forest.
I've steeped myself in such a sin,
help me Jesus to begin again
and let the cross
be the only tree
that my eyes and soul
will ever need,
Your life alone shows me how to be –
one who loves the forest
as well as every tree.

"Worship the Lord in the splendor of his holiness.
The voice of the Lord is over the waters..."
Psalm 29:2-3 NIV

I have silence
beside the sea
with only a cricket
for company
there is revelation
given to me
in creation's cathedral
made by Thee,
voiced by
speech not otherwise heard
declared to the earth,
to the uttermost world
it rises and sets
from end to end
Your knowledge beyond language
in what it sends -
the message that
Your precepts are right
proven by the witness
of Your radiant might
so let not my transgressions
rule over me
but let these meditations
be pleasing to Thee.

when I die
let me set sail
into the sunset
beyond travail
into the Lords' calming seas;
no great fanfare
but a fair winds breeze
drawing gently forward,
finally free,
toward the Lords'
outstretched hand
waiting,
reaching for me.

FALL 11

under Autumn's brooding skies
we give up walks
and turn inside
for harsher winds
are blowing in
another life is to begin
centered with a certainty
that for awhile
'tis how 'twill be
with scents of spice
and baking air
instead of meadows
flowers fair,
more wrapping up
and staying still,
compared to going
where we will,
so brooding too
we may embark
on changing times
that make their mark

Some of us cannot remit
from the deeper thoughts
but must submit
to the highs and lows –
the pendulum swings –
that beauty and sadness
together will bring.
Blessed are those
who continue to care
through the darkness
yet do not despair
and great is this God
who will carry us through
if we live for the Light
with thoughts
brought round to You.

FALL 12

while the sun is still shining,
I will turn over the soil for the season
for summer is waning fast
and the product of its reason
will hold us and last
through the long winter
while the splinter
of hope
that spring is certain and sure,
is why we turn the soil for the season,
Hope of God from
faith so pure

there is a harvest around us
if we but sow the seed
the Lord sends rain and sunshine
and all good things we need;
then comes the time of testing,
and faith as we would prepare
to keep eyes and mind both open,
to keep our souls aware
and watching for what
will transpire
through nights of prayer,
and days of trial,
until the time of harvest come
so thankful are we,
for suddenly,
as far as eye can see
the bountiful Truth
He's sent from above
is Lord, we are truly
surrounded by Your love!

FALL 13

I spend time in tears,
so much rendered
over the years;
all I can do is stand
and know the Love
that's lived through
God's command;
only with silence
and a setting apart
can such a mystery
come into the heart;
the Sacrifice of a
Holy Son,
best understood
when we are just one
and in His presence,
He presides
the filling of the soul,
where years of grief
can be set aside
and tears of happiness
fall from our eyes.

FALL 14

"Unless the LORD had been my help,
My soul would soon have settled in silence."
Psalm 94:17 NKJV

"Heal me, Lord, and I will be healed;
Save me and I will be saved,
For you are the one I praise."
Jeremiah 17:14 NIV

here we sit in silence be
in reverence
of Love from Thee
and know we have not
ever earned
what you have given
nor could return
the grace or goodness
given we,
in reverence
sit,
in silence be

I want to be like David,
a woman after God's own heart,
not that I take after Him
but that I'm after His deepest part.
Searching with my feelings,
singing with longing
through my songs,
I want to be like David
hoping for the heart of God
until my life is gone.

FALL 15

There's a God who cares for little girls
whose tears are seldom seen
who wonder why it's they who grieve
and what it all may mean?
Compassion falls on such as these
with the Father's tender hand,
He is reaching out to them,
one day they'll understand
there's a God who cares for little girls
whose tears are seldom seen
whom ministering angels gathered 'round
though they were never seen

Faith

the clouds today,
an obscuring smoke
o'er the fiery sun;
though unseen
yet it is not undone;
presiding over day,
returning without fail,
just knowing that it's there
brings all else to pale
as we feel its warmth
receiving, we,
give thanks whether
it's faith that we feel
or faith that we see

"In all their distress he too was distressed,
and the angel of his presence saved them.
In his love and mercy he redeemed them..."
Isaiah 63:9 NIV

FALL 16

hurting world
take hold of My hand
you try too hard
to understand -
faith will find its way
through these times
we can't control;
follow Me
I'll part the sea
you will make it through
'cause nothing less than Love
will be with you

FALL 17

"Jesus had compassion on them and
touched their eyes. Immediately they
received their sight and followed him."
Matthew 20:34 NIV

God who sees

cover us with Your feathers, oh Father,
brush the hair from my face,
let me lean against Your bosom
and know Your embrace;
for wounded we are
and suffering are we
longing for the True Love
and deep serenity;
promises you made,
we'll one day be,
under the wings
of the God who sees

FALL 18

"But Jesus came and touched them.
'Get up,' he said. 'Don't be afraid.'
When they looked up,
they saw no one except Jesus."
Matthew 17:7-8 NIV

girl of the fog
lost in the mist
though silence surrounds you
it will not persist
for outside your sight
there exists
the realm of the future
you cannot dismiss
for with it a hope
that won't be bound
by the droplet enclosure
encasing you now
with sight unfettered
full and free
revealed in God's time
with His Sovereignty

The only time I'll worry now
is when I'm on my knees
for there's no way to make things hurry
no way to take things at my ease,
for only God can shape the future
and only He is good,
He's the only one who controls it all
and the only one who should.

FALL 19

"They feast on the abundance of your house;
you give them drink from your river of delights.
For with you is the fountain of life;
in your light we see light."
Psalm 36:8-9 NIV

Was Jesus in His flesh
afraid
to look upon the cross
and know of its pain?
and did He in the garden dread
to such an extent
that drops of blood were shed
with agony He knew
would come
still able to say
"Thy will be done"
He shared with us in every way
our fears
our flesh
and yet He gave
the Love that none of us can give
through pain and death –
an eternity with God
to live!!!

the greatness of God
leaves us full of awe
as well and sure
that it should,
as He is Light
and the holder of Might
we bow to Him
who is good;
but maybe it's the meekness of Jesus
we'll meet
on that Golden Day,
to be glad that the Lord of eternity
is humble in His Holy way,
and instead of fear
we'll desire to draw near,
true kindness and mercy
we'll see,
to know in that place
Love in Jesus face
and sing praise through eternity.

"Look on my right hand and see,
For there is no one who acknowledges me;
Refuge has failed me;
No one cares for my soul."
Psalm 142:4 NKJV

Inside of me there's something missing,
a void that seldom cries –
so deep it's dormant,
resisting healing,
so in denial it lies
screaming for attention
yet too ashamed to rise
out into my daily living
for fear it be recognized.
But what you may never know
is how you filled a part
of my soul through your sharing
to bring healing to my heart.

In this world I wonder,
how much I'm supposed to give?
It seems an endless,
always more,
and life is hard to live.
Through each suffering
I have found
there's always come a dawn
leading me to finish each day
and Your grace to carry on,
so I pass the Truth of You
and what You will provide
to those who are in places dark
seeking a space to hide;
I'm certain, through faith,
when I've given it all
if I again fall
to despair,
I'll remember-
when I'm lifted to heaven,
You'll give only good to me there!

WINTER 21

when winter finds a home
and is welcomed there
the weather is relief
instead of despair;
where people rejoice
in the beauty that falls
a silence pervades
and yet it calls
and I answer-
clothed in the warmth
God provides
living with winter
in its home
outside

don't lose hope
and don't lose heart
you may be the only one
keeping someone apart
from ills unknown
and things unseen
keep up the courage
and remain where there's need

WINTER 22

*"Jesus said to him, 'You shall love the
LORD your God with all your heart, with
all your soul, and with all your mind.'"
Matthew 22:37 NKJV*

All doubts aside
Your grace will provide-
One must weather the winter
to appreciate the spring.
Only out from underneath
may Providence in true salvation bring
the restoration
from devastation
that can come from the One true King.
Oh listen, how the angels sing!
He is risen,
He's forgiven,
He has come beyond all telling
and all healing is His to bring.
Oh, hear the angels sing –
"Glory to God in the highest
and on earth, peace to men
on whom His favor rests."
Let there be no more doubting;
let's endure all tests.
His desire is but to keep the faith
let heaven open up its gates
for the flood of Love
is ready to escape
and fall upon each breathless heart
there is no more division
for He who has so given
has done so from His very heart.

WINTER 23

ice and snow
nowhere to go
that's not already in pain
yet they lead on a mission
comprised of a task
that's beyond themselves
and seldom ask -
"why?"
then the purpose appears-
people need saving
it is very clear
that love is essential
and never second hand
restoration is through revelation-
impossible to demand
taking place always within
yet we can only battle without
and pray that everything we give
will be turning their heads and hearts
from doubt

WINTER 24

this is not the last snow
I know
beauty is not at an end;
Love was given
doubt has been driven
from the heart as to what
He will yet send;
falling flakes
of perfect shape
accumulate
in a mantle of purity
to mend the heartbreak;
so I'll close my eyes,
trusting God and the skies
to send snow
and His Love,
knowing it be from He
and His,
in eternity,
to us from above.

WINTER 25

"The Lord is my strength and my shield;
my heart trusts in him and he helps me.
My heart leaps for joy,
and with my song I praise him."
Psalm 28:7 NIV

Consider the cardinal
all robed in red
rejoicing thru winter
and singing instead
of simply existing
for what lies ahead.
Granting each dawn
its chance for a day
where a hopeful song
may find its way
into the here
into the now
life is worth living,
we'll know it somehow,
for in each of us
the Creator has placed
a song
that belongs
to His sustaining grace.

I've given you a song;
a song of white
and a cardinal to share it with
in a tree within your sight;
you can, of course, just see all this,
or you can realize
I'm sending you My unfailing Love
to open up your eyes,
that from heaven is where
true Love flows –
you decide where it goes,
whether simply falling
to the ground
or becoming part
of heart and soul, bound;
you mean so much
that I've created this scene
just so you'll know
how much you mean
to Me
to Me
open your eyes child
and see!

WINTER 26

*"Israel put your hope in the Lord,
for with the Lord is unfailing love
and with him is full redemption."
Psalm 130:7 NIV*

*"My soul faints with longing for your salvation,
But I have put my hope in your word.
Psalm 119:81*

WINTER 27

*"Hearing of this, the crowds followed
him on foot from the towns. When Jesus
landed and saw a large crowd,
he had compassion on them
and healed their sick."*
Matthew 14:13-14 NIV

lay it all down-
the busy hands,
the unfruitful mind,
turning over and over again
and find
that God is willing-
even desires-
to take of our worries
and that which tires
as He knows we are dust,
that the burdens we bear
aren't even ours
if we know that He cares
to take it all
as if thrown upon the wind

the Holy Spirit comes and flows
to take it away
we know not where it goes;
maybe the eye can't see
but His wind we will hear
as His Love He will send
to the burdened and
those held dear.

WINTER 28

When it is winter
let me think of the spring
for there is peace
in the remembering
when life was new
and all was green
so much sadness
still unseen;
all that goodness
still remains
a part of me –
I hear the strains
of comforting birds
and sunshine's rays
in peacefulness on
the grassy plain
where kind folks' dwell
just over the hill –
no matter the winter,
I'll live there still.

WINTER 29

"In the multitude of my anxieties within me,
Your comforts delight my soul."
Psalm 94:19 NKJV

Assurance Seeds

Such a difficult time of year
the snow is slow to disappear,
it struggles to hang on;
the life beneath
strains to appear
wishing it all were gone.
Creatures reach inside themselves
sustained with a final drive to spring
while humans deal with winter's ills
and to life's promise cling.
So, we'll set our sights ahead
to look with faith and hope instead
of past struggles,
looking for the strength we need
lying in God's assurance seeds.

"But while he was still a long way off,
his father saw him and was filled with
compassion for him; he ran to his son,
threw his arms around him and kissed him."
Luke 15:20 NIV

WINTER 30

When the snow fields soften
the birds begin to sing,
the trees stretch out awakening arms
as buds turn emerald green.
The sun lays long on sodden land
and bids the seed to grow,
returning earth to harbor man,
to nourish and to sow.
So take me in and shelter me
from winter harsh and sad,
and carry me along with Thee
a springtime heart
and glad...

SPRING 31

Begin sweet Jesus
to sweep over me
like the changing of the seasons
like the waves upon the sea
move through my emotions
You will bring
the newness of Your saving grace
the freshness of the spring
come to us
though we be still
and carry us
into Your will
taken away
with loving care
swept up in Your Spirit
my deliverance
there

I want to rest in a melody
that I have never known
and drift upon its lifting wings
wherever they are blown
trusting it will carry me
to peaceful places yet unseen
where health and healing
like a musical brook
mingle with birdsong
to form a prayer book

SPRING 32

Barefoot girl out in the grass
has no idea how time should pass,
way beyond her hour to return from play,
"The butterflies were too beautiful today."

Sitting in class as the teacher talked,
looking at the meadow, past the sidewalk,
when asked to answer, all she could say -
"The butterflies are so beautiful today."

Next she's walking down the aisle,
seeing nothing but her intended's smile,
she's giving a glow that made everyone say-
"How beautiful the bride is today."

Her husband came home to a mess again,
the house looks like a big play pen,
she sighs as she answers in a gentle way -
"The baby was just too beautiful today."

Time flew by, how quickly it went,
her arms grow weak, her energies spent,
but this lady noticed, all along the way,
how beautiful the butterflies were –
each day.

SPRING 33

"My soul finds rest in God alone;
my salvation comes from him."
Psalm 62:1 NIV

We're part of His masterpiece;
the beauty of nature
the grandeur of the sky
we've been placed here just as intentionally
you and I.
No mistakes
and no regrets,
as purposeful a meaning
as any life can get.
Every soul should take comfort
that the Divine
never ceases His loving,
He wants you to shine,
no matter how high
no matter how low
your feeling of yourself
may go,
God has known your thoughts
and still
you're here and that means
you're a part of His will
to remain
continually looking on high,
you're a part of His masterpiece
and precious in His eye.

SPRING 34

"...from the first day that you set
your heart to understand,
and to humble yourself before your God,
your words were heard..."
Daniel 10:12 NKJV

I am human –
my mind is small;
much of what it wraps around
is of no significance at all.
Daily, I speak the language
of earth and of mankind
so when my heart is heavy
and feels so confined –
I open up in prayer
like a flower in the spring
no boundaries can ever contain
this purest of offerings,
soaring far beyond the sky
yet intimately told –
the simplest words of a loving prayer
change the seasons of the soul.

The wind through the curtains
time unseen;
flowing past,
what does it mean?
To sit in the chair
my grandfather sat
so long ago
bringing memories back
with merging of feelings
time comes together
as if ends were meeting
and a day were forever...
maybe a lifetime
is but one page
the script runs together
regardless of age
like a flower blooming
a continuous flow
maturing then fading
after it's grown...
the breezes keep coming
as the earth turns round
yet I'll live in this moment
so rich, so profound...

SPRING 35

"Heal me, LORD, and I will be healed;
save me and I will be saved,
for you are the one I praise."
Jeremiah 17:14 NIV

In times of want,
in drought of soul,
when life itself –
beyond control,
that is when we
learn to see –
who is watching over me?
Beyond all doubt,
when in despair,
we live without
and turn to prayer,
that is when
we beg to see–
who is watching over me?
And when survived,
the effort's made
to share or hide
that which was prayed,
that is when–
acknowledge we,
He who watches over me...

SPRING 36

*"For my Father's will is that
everyone who looks to the Son
and believes in him shall have eternal life,
and I will raise them up at the last day."
John 6:40 NIV*

Overture to eternity

When I get to heaven will I say –
this is the healing music I heard
while on earth
when my soul was so disturbed;
and this is the warmth
that came my way
when no one knew what to do or to say;
it is all here and it's come to pass
that faith in You
held steadfast,
was Your coming to me
and an overture to eternity.
The feeling of being held
was Your Spirit that swelled
inside of one who now can see
all that You are
is exactly what You said you would be.

SPRING 37

Who is this
transforming power
turning misery to mercy
at the ninth hour?
Here He is
as humble as a lamb
adhering to His love for us –
truly the great "I Am".
His misery is mingling
with mine
only He is truly
the Divine!
Son of God the Father
He has come to take it all
He was as burdened
as certain
as I am flawed.
I cannot fathom
His love
to take
my torment and wrongs,
He who made no mistake,
who gave only goodness
on this earth of lament
but because of His sacrifice
He would prevent
any more suffering –
by His ascent

and turn misery to mercy
as was His Almighty intent.
Praise the Lord, Praise the Lord
for now and forever more – Praise the Lord!

"The eternal God is your refuge,
And underneath are the everlasting arms."
Deuteronomy 33:27 NKJV

SPRING 38

One day I –
a daughter will be
given a crown
because of the King,
something of which I never earned
but was called upon
only then to learn
all of the freedom
and power bequeathed
from a Sovereign God
who took me from beneath
and from His throne
too far away to see
He's continued to love
and look after me
until the day
I rise to meet
the One in power
who, in kindness,
from His seat,
tells me I'm a daughter
and part of His family
born to life through Jesus His Son
and forever
together
we will all be as one.

SPRING 39

the Son that radiates within,
there is no end
no place to begin,
He is in all
and through
His eternal voice of Love says
"I will never leave you".
Life sweeps past,
an icy blast,
of the world
and its cruelty
presenting itself
for each of us
differently.
But You are always here
resonant and true
Your eternal voice of Love says
"I will never leave you".
A place of peace,
so let it rest,
inside my soul
that You know best
and underneath
this continual cry
the constant comfort
of reassurance lies-
Christ came for me,
You'll never let go,

it was for me
Your Love was shown
that nothing
in heaven or earth
can move
the words You spoke
"I will never leave you".

"I will never leave you or forsake you."
Hebrews 13:5 NKJV

SPRING 40

"For the Lord Himself will descend from heaven with a voice of an archangel...And the dead in Christ will rise first. Then we who are alive and remain shall be caught up together with them in the clouds to meet the Lord... And thus we shall always be with the Lord. Therefore comfort one another with these words."
1 Thess. 4:16-18 NKJV

Return to Eden

The faint stirrings
of light and birdsong
signal the morn,
just as in Eden –
a new day is born.
Shafts of sun
through drifting mist
as the forest floor was lit
to comfort human spirit
with gentle assurance
our eyes would upward lift...
oh, to have lived a single day
with such communion and in such bliss;
surely His salvation to us all
holds a return to such as this.

Printed in the United States
by Baker & Taylor Publisher Services